Eberhard Arnold

Why
we live in
community

with two interpretive talks by

Thomas Merton

foreword by
Basil Pennington

 Plough Publishing House

Published by Plough Publishing House
Walden, New York
Robertsbridge, England
Elsmore, Australia
www.plough.com

Why We Live in Community is a translation of *Warum wir in Gemeinschaft leben*, an
essay published in Eberhard Arnold's journal *Die Wegwarte* I:10/11 (October/November
1925) and again in III:8/9 (May/June 1927), in Sannerz, Germany.

1st English Edition: 1967
2nd English Edition:1976
3rd English Edition: 1995

ISBN 10: 0-87486-068-7
ISBN 13: 978-0-87486-068-9

20 19 18 17 16 15 14   12 11 10 9 8 7 6

A catalog record for this book is available from the British Library.
Library of Congress Cataloging-in-Publication Data
Arnold, Eberhard, 1883–1935.
   Why we live in community / Eberhard Arnold : with two interpretive talks by Thomas
Merton : edited by the Bruderhof. – 3rd English ed.
      p. cm.
   "Why we live in community is a translation of Warum wir in Gemeinschaft leben, an
essay published in Eberhard Arnold's journal Die Wegwarte I:10/11 (October/November
1925) and again in III: 8/9 (May/June 1927), in Sannerz, Germany"–T.p. verso.
   Includes bibliographical references.
   ISBN 0-87486-068-7 (pbk.)
   1. Bruderhof–Doctrines. 2. Christian communities. 3. Christianity and culture. 4.
Christianity and politics. 5. Nonviolence–Religious aspects–Christianity. I. Merton,
Thomas, 1915-1968. II. Bruderhof (Rifton, N.Y.) III. Title.
BX8129.B65A74 1995
289. 7'3–dc20   95-18007
   CIP

Printed in the USA

Contents

We do not want you to copy or imitate us. We want to be like a ship that has crossed the ocean, leaving a wake of foam, which soon fades away. We want you to follow the Spirit, which we have sought to follow, but which must be sought anew in every generation.

First generation Quakers
at Balby, York, late 17th century

Foreword
by Basil Pennington

There is something stark about Eberhard Arnold's statement on community. It is chiseled clearly in the solid granite of faith. It does not spare us any of the anguish of a world so horribly failing in community – even communities of faith. Our open wounds confront us. Arnold stands unambiguously in the church's option for the poor, the option of our divine Founder. For him, community is our way of saying an existential "yes" to God and his creation, to our own nature and predestination, a predestination, though, that will only come about – by God's own design – if we work for it and work together.

In a world where the gulf between the haves and the have-nots is growing ever wider we need to again be forcefully and persistently confronted with the ideals of the early Christian community. It is certainly a scandal when a person who professes to be a disciple of Jesus goes off to his bed well fed, and with food in his larder, while a fellow human hungers within his reach. It is certainly a scandal when a person professes to be a disciple of Jesus and uses his God-given talents only to augment his own wealth—while fathers cry out for an opportunity to earn a living for their children. Perhaps the ecclesial communities would more effectively enlighten such benighted consciences if they reformed and renewed the powerful sacramentality which Arnold reminds us of.

It may be difficult for today's Christians to hear Arnold's constant reminder that the fullness of life, which is found only in community, comes at the cost of complete self-sacrifice. Yet that is the Paschal mystery of life through death. And it is a sacrifice shot through with joy. Arnold brings out the real paradox that is so essential for the vibrant community, but so difficult to attain: the requirement that each member lives out a personal decision to surrender to the whole and yet exercises his or her will for the good. The secret behind this is, of course, the Holy Spirit, a secret a faithless world cannot know—hence the many strivings for community that end in shambles, with deeply wounded people feeling totally betrayed. A community animated with the Spirit centers on Christ by necessity; it knows the struggle for liberation in Christ, and so it lives in the hope of the resurrection. It is a community of universal love, a leaven in the human family. The Spirit enters into a community when, through its members' common yearning, the community opens itself and makes itself ready to be Spirit-driven.

Arnold speaks out of the spirit of the Reformation when he issues a call to "those who are called," and his call echoes the call of Augustine, Benedict, Bernard, Francis, Ignatius, and Don Bosco. Anyone knowing how the life of the church has been continually enriched by these charismatic leaders and the communities which they founded (and which they continue to inspire across the centuries) cannot but feel some regret that their legacy has not been cherished more. Christian communities living in this time of vital renewal will draw rich inspiration from Arnold's penetrating analysis of what community animated by the Spirit really calls us to.

It is precisely this that Thomas Merton was trying to help the Sisters at Precious Blood Monastery in Alaska—and all of us who read his words—to do. As genial a person as Merton was—and he was certainly a very down-to-earth monk—he was also a genius. With penetrating lucidity, he captures and sets forth the essence of Arnold's thought. Merton summons us with Arnold, Gandhi, and Martin Luther King to the higher plan of the Spirit, to the realm of love— not to an ideal, but to the real, practical love these men lived and died for.

Merton's thought in his two published talks on Arnold is wide-ranging. Placing Arnold in historical context with incisive clarity, he then proceeds to make extensive verbatim use of the latter's masterly essay. He does not hesitate to make criticisms in the few cases where he feels Arnold has overstated his case, but he immediately goes on to qualify them by showing us the validity of Arnold's underlying insight and his ultimate conclusion. Like Arnold, Merton is totally Christocentric, and we can only admire his comprehensive grasp of Pauline Christology and the ease with which he weaves it into his exposition. He proclaims in very straight-forward language the fact that community is love's victory over death, lived – by *ordinary* people – in union with Christ, by the grace of his victory.

Both Merton and Arnold emphasize that ordinary people can live the victory of community, though not by their own doing; it is possible only through God's working in and among them. We need to see this very clearly. If we do not, we cannot face the evil in us that militates against community. We let it discourage us, and we give up in our attempt to live communally, or we repress it and relate in a superficial and untruthful way that never realizes true community. It is poor, weak, stupid sinners that Christ finds his joy and glory in bringing to loving oneness through the activity of his Spirit. As Merton says, "The ultimate thing is that we build community not on our love but on God's love." In the midst of conflict, our question should not be "Who is right?"

but "Do we believe?" "Faith is first, and the only one who is right is God."

I am sure Arnold would only feel joy that the leading Catholic writer of this century was so completely in harmony with him in his thinking, a harmony that spilled over into life as Merton lived the age-old traditional monastic life that for celibates incorporates all the values and ideals that Arnold held so precious and essential to true Christian community. How well Merton resonated to Arnold's hymn of labor and the simple life – this monk who belonged to an order that defined itself as characterized by the spirit of simplicity.

When we see spiritual giants like Thomas Merton and Eberhard Arnold reach across what in times past seemed to be an unbridgeable gap, we are not only inspired; we see how and why we have come as far as we have today, and we may take courage to dream dreams we dared not dream before. Because prophetic figures throughout the ages have dared to proclaim "I have a dream," we, too, have a dream – a dream that is being realized. We have a long way yet to go, but it is solid food for the journey like this bread Arnold first served in the wilderness that gives us the strength to press on toward the mark: the full realization of human solidarity in Christ Jesus. For we are compelled by Jesus' own Spirit, who breathes deeply and gives utterance through the impelling words of men who were not afraid to lay themselves totally open to that uncontrollable Spirit.

Basil Pennington
April 1995

Eberhard Arnold

Why we live in community

Why community?

Life in community is no less than a necessity for us – it is an inescapable "must" that determines everything we do and think. Yet it is not our good intentions or efforts that have been decisive in our choosing this way of life. Rather, we have been overwhelmed by a certainty – a certainty that has its origin and power in the Source of everything that exists. We acknowledge God as this Source.

We must live in community because all life created by God exists in a communal order and works toward community.

Faith is our basis

God is the source of life. On him and through him our common life is built up and led time and again through cataclysmic struggles to final victory. It is an exceedingly dangerous way, a way of deep suffering. It is a way that leads straight into the struggle for existence and the reality of a life of work, into all the difficulties created by the human character. And yet, just this is our deepest joy: to see clearly the eternal struggle – the indescribable tension between life and death, man's position between heaven and hell – and still to believe in the overwhelming power of life, the power of love to overcome, and the triumph of truth, because we believe in God.

This faith is not a theory for us; neither is it a dogma, a system of ideas, or a fabric of words, nor a cult or an organization. Faith means receiving God himself – it means being overwhelmed by God. Faith is the strength that enables us to go this way. It helps us to find trust again and again when, from a human point of view, the foundations of trust have been destroyed. Faith gives us the vision to perceive what is essential and eternal. It gives us eyes to see what cannot be seen, and hands to grasp what cannot be touched, although it is present always and everywhere.

If we possess faith, we will no longer judge people in the light of social custom or according to their weaknesses, for we will see the lie that stands behind all the masks of our mammonistic, unclean, and murderous human society. Yet we will not be deceived in the other direction either and made to think that the maliciousness and fickleness of the human character (though factual) are its real and ultimate nature. Admittedly, with our present nature, without God, we humans are incapable of community. Temperamental mood-swings, possessive impulses and cravings for physical and emotional satisfaction, powerful currents of ambition and touchiness, the desire for personal influence over others, and human privileges of all kinds—all these place seemingly insurmountable obstacles in the way of true community. But with faith we cannot be deluded into thinking that these realities are decisive: in the face of the power of God and his all-conquering love, they are of no significance. God is stronger than these realities. The unifying energy of his Spirit overcomes them all.

Here it becomes abundantly clear that the realization of true community, the actual building up of a communal life, is impossible without faith in a higher Power. In spite of all that goes wrong, people try again and again to put their trust either in human goodness (which really does exist) or in the force of law. But all their efforts are bound to come to grief when faced with the reality of evil. The only power that can build true community is faith in the ultimate mystery of the Good, faith in God.

We must live in community because only in such a positive venture can it become clear how incapable of life unredeemed man is, and what a life-giving and community-building power God is.

Community answers the social-political question

There are political organizations that stand, as we do, for international peace, the abolition of private property, and full community of goods. Yet we cannot simply side with these organizations and fight their battles in their way. We do feel drawn, with them, to all people who suffer need and distress, to those who lack food and shelter and whose very mental development is stunted through exploitation. With them, we stand side by side with the "have-nots," with the underprivileged, and with the degraded and oppressed. And yet we avoid the kind of class struggle that employs violent means to avenge lives taken through exploitation. We reject the defensive war of the suppressed just as much as the defensive wars of nations.

We must live in community because we take our stand in the spiritual fight on the side of all those who fight for freedom, unity, peace, and social justice.

Community is the answer of faith

All revolutions, all communes and idealistic or reform-oriented movements, force us to recognize again and again that one thing alone can quicken our faith in the Good: the clear example of action born of truth, when both action and word are one in God. We have only one weapon against the depravity that exists today – the weapon of the Spirit, which is constructive work carried out in the fellowship of love. We do not acknowledge sentimental love, love without work. Nor do we acknowledge dedication to practical work if it does not daily give proof of a heart-to-heart relationship between those who work together, a relationship that comes from the Spirit. The love of work, like the work of love, is a matter of the Spirit. The love that comes from the Spirit is work.

When working men and women voluntarily join hands to renounce everything that is self-willed, isolated, or private, their alliances become signposts to the ultimate unity of all people, which is found in God's love and in the power of his coming kingdom. The will that works toward this kingdom of peace for all, like the ungrudging spirit of brotherliness in work, comes from God. Work as spirit and spirit as work – that is the fundamental nature of the future order of peace, which comes to us in Christ. Work alone makes it possible to live in community, for work means joy in striving for the common good and joy in the presence of those we strive with. Such joy is given to us only as far as we are able to sustain a consecrated relationship to the Eternal, even when performing the most mundane tasks – only as far as we remember that everything that is material and earthly is, at the same time, consecrated to God's future.

We must live in community because God wants us to respond to the unclear longings of our time with a clear answer of faith.

Community through the history of the church

The spirit-filled life of love that arises from faith has been decisively witnessed to over the centuries, especially by the Jewish prophets and later by the first Christians. We acknowledge Christ, the historical Jesus, and with him his entire message as proclaimed by his apostles and practiced by his followers. Therefore we stand as brothers and sisters with all those who have joined together to live in community through the long course of history. They appeared among the Christians of the first century; in the prophetic movement of the Montanists in the second; in the monasticism of the following centuries; in the revolutionary movement of justice and love led by Arnold of Brescia; in the Waldensian movement; in the itinerant communities of Francis of Assisi; among the Bohemian and Moravian Brethren and the Brothers of the Common Life; among the Beguines and Beghards; in the Anabaptist movements of the sixteenth century; among the early Quakers; among the Labadists of the seventeenth and eighteenth centuries; among the early Moravians, and in many other denominations and movements down to our present day.

We must live in community because we are compelled by the same Spirit that has led to community time and again since the days of biblical prophecy and early Christianity.

Life in community means life in the Spirit

Community in the early church   We acknowledge Jesus and early Christianity. The early Christians dedicated themselves as much to people's outward needs as to their inner ones. Jesus brought life: he healed sick bodies, resurrected the dead, drove out demons from tormented souls, and carried his message of joy to the poorest of the poor.

Jesus' message means the realization of the future invisible kingdom now; it is the promise that ultimately the earth will be won wholly for God.

It is the whole that matters here. Just as the love of God does not acknowledge any boundary or stop at any barrier, Jesus does not stop in the face of property any more than he does in the face of theology, moralism, or the State. Jesus saw into the heart of the rich young man, whom he loved, and said, "One thing you lack: sell all you have, give it to the poor, and come with me!" It was a matter of course for Jesus that his disciples should hold no personal possessions but rather keep a common purse. Only one man was entrusted with the hateful responsibility of managing the disciples' money, and he broke under it – a lesson with no little significance for our mammonistic society today.

Yet even Christ's betrayal and execution did not mean defeat. The enthusiastic experience of the Spirit with which the Risen One endowed his itinerant disciples gave them the power to carry on their communal life on a larger scale. The first church became a community of several thousand people who, because love was burning in them, had to stay together. In all questions regarding communal life, the forms that emerged were in keeping with an understanding of life as one unified whole.

The first Christians in Jerusalem held everything in common. Whoever owned property felt compelled from within to share it. No one had anything that did not belong to the church. Yet what the church owned was there for all. Its generous love excluded no one, and an open door and an open heart were therefore among its characteristics. At the time of its flowering it found ways to reach all people. And though its members were bound to become the target of hatred and hostility, they still won the love and trust of those around them. It was inevitable that they should, for they were there heart and soul for everyone.

Community today   The early Christians lived in the Spirit. The Spirit blows like the wind – it is never rigid like iron or stone. The Spirit is infinitely more sensitive and delicate than the inflexible designs of the intellect or the cold, hard framework of governmental or societal structures. The Spirit is more sensitive even than all the emotions of the human soul, more sensitive than all the powers of the human heart, on which people so often try – in vain – to build lasting edifices. But just for this reason the Spirit is stronger and more irresistible than all these things, never to be overcome by any power, however terrible; for it is the breadth, depth, and height of being.

In Jesus, who lived a life of love without violence, love without rights, and love without the desire to possess, the Spirit lives on powerfully as the Risen One, as the inner voice and the inner eye that leads to community.

The light of the early church illuminated the path of humankind in only one short flash. Yet its spirit and witness stayed alive even after its members had been scattered and many of them murdered. Again and again through history, similar forms arose as gifts of God, expressions of the same living Spirit. Witnesses were killed, and fathers died, but new children were–and are– born to the Spirit again and again. Communities pass away. But the church that creates them remains.

Efforts to organize community artificially can only result in ugly, lifeless caricatures. Only when we are empty and open to the Living One–to the Spirit–can he bring about the same life among us as he did among the early Christians. The Spirit is joy in the Living One, joy in God as the only real life; it is joy in all people, because they have life from God. The Spirit drives us to all people and brings us joy in living and working for one another, for it is the spirit of creativity and love.

Community life is possible only in this all-embracing Spirit and in those things it brings with it: a deepened spirituality and the ability to experience life more keenly and intensely. Surrendering to this Spirit is such a powerful experience that we can never feel equal to it. In truth, the Spirit alone is equal to itself. It quickens our energies by firing the inmost core – the soul of the community – to white heat. When this core burns and blazes to the point of sacrifice, it radiates far and wide.

Community life is like martyrdom by fire: it means the daily sacrifice of all our strength and all our rights, all the claims we commonly make on life and assume to be justified. In the symbol of fire the individual logs burn away so that, united, its glowing flames send out warmth and light again and again into the land.

We must live in community because the spirit of joy and love gives us such an urge to reach out to others that we wish to be united with them for all time.

The symbolism of community

Community as a pattern in nature The whole of life, with all the various forms it takes in nature, is a parable of the future community of the kingdom. Just as the air surrounds us, or as a blowing wind engulfs us, we need to be immersed in the blowing Spirit, who unites and renews everything. And just as water washes and cleanses us every day, so in the deep symbol of baptism by immersion we witness to our purification from everything that is of death. This "burial" in water, which happens only once, signifies a complete break from the status quo; it is a vow of mortal enmity toward the evil in us and around us. Similarly, the lifting out of the water, which also happens only once, proclaims resurrection in vivid imagery and in unforgettable clarity.

The resurrection we see everywhere in nature is no different: after the dying of autumn and winter comes the blossoming of spring and the fruit-bearing of summer; after seedtime comes harvest. In fact, the whole course of human history, from man's origins to his final fulfillment, is symbolized by the cycle of nature.

Symbolism can be found in the trivialities of existence, too: when approached with reverence, even daily rites such as mealtimes can become consecrated festivals of community. On a deeper level, we find the expression of community in the symbol of the Lord's Supper: the meal of wine and bread. The Meal of Remembrance not only witnesses to the catastrophe of Christ's death and to his second coming, but to the fact that we receive him in ourselves. It witnesses to his church – his Body – as the ultimate unity of life.

Community as a body   The twofold symbol of the body endowed with a soul – of the indwelling of the Spirit in creation – is visible in every human being in a uniquely pointed way. It acquires special meaning in the unity of two people in marriage; for as a bond of faithfulness of one man and one woman, marriage is a picture not only of the unity of the Spirit with humankind, but also of Christ with his church. In marriage, purity – the tempered self-discipline of the sex life – becomes liberating joy in created life.

In the human body, community is maintained only by the constant cycle of dying cells being replaced by new ones. In a similar way, a life of full community can take shape as an organism only where there is heroic sacrifice. Because it is an educational fellowship of mutual help and correction, of shared resources, and of work, a true community is a covenant made in free-willing surrender and sacrifice. As such it fights for the existence of the church.

In the context of church community, justice does not consist in making and satisfying even reasonable demands for personal rights; on the contrary, it consists in giving each member the opportunity to risk everything, to surrender himself completely so that God may become incarnate in him and so that the kingdom may break into his life with power. This cannot take place in the form of hard demands made on others, however, but in joyous self-sacrifice—for God's Spirit comes to expression as cheerfulness and courage in making sacrifices; as free-willingness; as delight in work, joy in people, and dedication to the whole. Joy and enthusiasm take shape as active love.

We love the body because it is a consecrated dwelling place of the Spirit. We love the soil because God's Spirit spoke and created the earth, and because he called it out of its uncultivated natural state so that it might be cultivated by the communal work of man. We love physical work—the work of muscle and hand—and we love the craftsman's art, in which the spirit guides the hand. In the way spirit and hand work through each other we see the mystery of community.

We love the activity of mind and spirit, too: the richness of all the creative arts and the exploration of the intellectual and spiritual interrelationships in history and in humanity's destiny of peace. Whatever our work, we must recognize and do the will of God in it. God—the creative

Spirit—has formed nature, and he has entrusted the earth to us, his sons and daughters, as an inheritance but also as a task: our garden must become his garden, and our work must further his kingdom.

We must live in community because we are stimulated by the same creative Spirit of unity who calls nature to unity and through whom work and culture shall become community in God.

Community is a sign of the coming kingdom

No less significant than the symbol of the Body is the symbol of community as the harbinger of God's kingdom—as the news that God will triumph over the earth. When God reigns there will be joy and peace and justice. In the same way as each individual living body consists of millions of independent cells, humankind will become one organism. This organism already exists today in the invisible church.

When we acknowledge the reality of this invisible church's unity and order, we acknowledge at the same time the freedom of the Spirit within that order. The more clearly a community defines its unique task, the more deeply conscious it must be of belonging to the *una sancta*, the One Church. Because it is part of a larger organism, it needs the give-and-take that comes from serving the whole Body, and it needs to be instructed and guided by the united witness of all those who believe in the church.

Self-determination – and self-surrender The
secret of community lies in the freedom of self-
determination, in the personal decision of each
member to surrender to the whole and, at the
same time, to exercise his will for the good. This
freedom, without which communal life cannot exist, is not a matter of power exercised by
human self-will, just as little as it is a matter of
spinelessness or unrestraint. In a community of
deeply moved people who believe in the Spirit,
the freedom of the individual lives in the free
decision of the united will brought about by the
Spirit. Working from within each member as the
will for the good, freedom becomes unanimity
and concord. The will of a man or woman liber-
ated in this way will be directed toward the kingdom, toward God's unity, and toward the good
of the whole human race. As such it becomes
life's most vital and intense energy.

Standing as it does in a world of death, an active will must constantly assert itself against
the destructive and enslaving powers of lying,
impurity, capitalism, and military force. It is

engaged in battle everywhere: against the spirit of murder, against all hostility (including the venom of the taunting, quarrelling tongue), against all the wrong and injustice people do to each other. That is, it fights in public as well as in private life against the very nature of hatred and death, and against all that opposes community. The call to freedom is a call to a battle without pause, a war without respite. Those who are called to it must be continually alert. They need not only the greatest willpower they themselves can muster, but also the aid of every other power yielded them by God, in order to meet the plight of the oppressed, to stand with the poor, and to fight against all evil in themselves and in the world around them.

This fight against evil must be waged more strongly within a community than against the world outside, but it must be waged even more relentlessly within each individual. In community, it is fought by the spirit of the church, which takes its foothold in each individual and fights the old Adam within him from the position of the new. In this way all softness, all flabby indulgence, is overcome by the burning power of love.

We must live in community because the struggle of life against death demands united ranks of souls and bodies that can be mobilized wherever death threatens life.

Community of goods   Community of goods presupposes the willingness of each individual member to turn over unconditionally to the common household whatever he acquires in the way of income or property, large or small. Yet even the community does not regard itself as the corporate owner of its inventory and enterprises. Rather, it acts as a trustee of the assets it holds for the common good of all, and for this reason it keeps its door open to all. By the same token it requires for its decision-making undisturbed unanimity in the Spirit.

Loyalty to the end   It is clear that the war of liberation for unity and for the fullness of love is being fought on many fronts with many different weapons. So too, the work of community finds expression in many different ways because the Spirit is rich. But there is a certainty of purpose for every stretch of the way we are called to go, and when we possess this certainty we will be given the strength for loyalty and unerring clarity, even in small things, to the very end. Nothing can be entrusted to the person who cannot hold out. Only those who stand firm can bear the standard.

Subordination to the whole   There is no great commission without a specific, clearly defined task. Yet it is of decisive importance that any special task lead only to Christ – that it truly serve the whole, the church, the coming kingdom. Wherever people see their task as something special in itself, they will go astray. But when a person serves the whole, even if in his special place and in his own particular way, he can well say, "I belong to God and to life in community," or to God and to any other calling.

Before our human service can become divine service, however, we must recognize how small and limited it is in the face of the whole.

A special calling – living in community, for instance – must never be confused with the church of Christ itself. Life in community means discipline in community, education in community, and continual training for the discipleship of Christ. Yet the mystery of the church is something different from this – something greater. It is God's life, and coming from him it penetrates community. This penetration of the divine into the human occurs whenever the tension of desperate yearning produces an openness and readiness in which God alone may act and speak. At such moments a community can be commissioned by the invisible church and given certainty for a specific mission: to speak and act – albeit without mistaking itself for the church – in the name of the church.

Community is a call to love and unity

The church we believe in lives in the Holy Spirit. The Spirit we believe in bears the church within itself. This church of the Spirit will give life to the future unity of humankind. It gives life already now to all truly living communities. The foundation and basic element of every community is not merely the combination of its members but simply and solely the unity of the Holy Spirit, for the true church is present there.

An organism becomes a unit through the unity of consciousness brought about by the spirit that animates it. It is the same in a believing community. The future unity of humankind, when God alone will rule, is ensured by the Holy Spirit. For this Spirit is the coming leader and Lord himself. The only thing we can hold on to here and now, the only thing we can already perceive of this great future of love and unity, is the Spirit. Faith in the Spirit is faith in the church and faith in the kingdom.

Community means sacrifice

In the life of a community, several decisive questions will need to be confronted again and again: how are we called? to what are we called? will we follow the call? Only a few are called to the special way that is ours. Yet those who are called—a small, battle-tried band, who must sacrifice themselves again and again—will hold firmly for the rest of their lives to the common task shown them by God. They will be ready to sacrifice life itself for the sake of unity.

People tear themselves away from home, parents, and career for the sake of marriage; for the sake of wife and child they risk their lives. In the same way it is necessary to break away and sacrifice everything for the sake of our calling to this way. Our witness to voluntary community of goods and work, to a life of peace and love, will have meaning only when we throw our entire life and livelihood into it.

Community – an adventure of faith

It is over five [now seventy-five] years since our tiny fellowship in Berlin decided to venture, in the sense of this confession, to live and work together in community on a basis of trust. With time, a life of total community came into being.

We are small in number, we come from the most diverse backgrounds and walks of life, but we want to place ourselves as one group in the service of all people.

Given our basis of faith, we cannot approach the development of our community from a purely economic point of view. We cannot simply select the most capable people for our various work departments. We aim for efficiency in all areas; but far more important, we seek faith. Each of us – whether committed member, helper, or guest – must be faced again and again with the question whether or not he is growing into the coming community ruled by Christ, no matter what his special service or task.

Our work, then, is a venture dared again and again. Yet we are not the driving force in this—it is we who have been driven and who must be urged on. The danger of exhaustion and uselessness is always present, but it is continually overcome by the faith that underlies mutual help.

Thomas Merton

Two interpretive talks

on Eberhard Arnold's
Why we live in community

Thomas Merton gave his two talks "Building Community on God's Love" and "Community, Politics, and Contemplation" in September 1968 at the Monastery of the Precious Blood in Eagle River, Alaska. Merton's extensive verbatim quotations from the 1967 edition of "Why We Live In Community" have been replaced here by corresponding passages from the 1995 edition above.

Building community on God's love

Eberhard Arnold wrote "Why We Live in Community" in the 1920s, at a time of great tension. It is a fine gospel statement of community against the background of false community being spread in his day. It may also be seen against the background of the present mystique of community. As you know, there is quite a strong trend among progressive believers towards the concept of real community. Eberhard Arnold comes out with what I think is a completely Christian answer. But before we start considering our vocation and our life, we have to stop and think what our Lord was doing. What did he come into the world for? What did he die on the cross for? What was his aim? Because that necessarily affects our aim, and it affects what we are doing.

The standard answer always used to be, "He came to die for sinners." That is to say, we are converted from sin; we don't have to go to hell; we can go to heaven if we behave ourselves. And that is a really crude answer, because there is so much more in it than that. Our Lord came to overcome death by love, and this work of love was a work of obedience to the Father unto death—a total gift of himself in order to overcome death. That is our job. We are fighting death; we are involved in a struggle between love and death, and this struggle takes place in each of us. Our Lord's victory over death, the victory of love over death on the cross, seeks to be manifested in a very concrete form on earth in the creation of community. The work of creating community in and by the grace of Christ is the place where this struggle goes on and where he manifests his victory over death.

Let's take a quick look at Saint Paul. There may be many better quotations on this point, but this is about us—we are chosen for this life, yet we are just ordinary people, people with our own limitations, as Saint Paul stresses in the famous passage of 1 Cor. 1:26–31:

> Take yourselves for instance, brothers, at the time when you were called: how many of you

were wise in the ordinary sense of the word, how many were influential people, or came from noble families?

The old text was: "Consider your vocation" – consider this fact: who are we who are called to share in the work of Christ, the superhuman work of overcoming death?

> No, it was to shame the wise that God chose what is foolish by human reckoning; those whom the world thinks common and contemptible are the ones that God has chosen – those who are nothing at all to show up those who are everything. The human race has nothing to boast about to God, but you, God has made members of Christ Jesus and by God's doing he has become our wisdom, and our virtue, and our holiness, and our freedom. As Scripture says: *if anyone wants to boast, let him boast about the Lord.*

So, here we are in this job of building community, which is what Christ died for, and whom does he pick to build community? He picks us, just ordinary people with ordinary weaknesses.

Some of the people who have come to Gethse-mani[1] with the best minds don't have vocations; often the ones who do have vocations are the ones who are always going to struggle along with their weaknesses and the ordinary problems of life. We must take this for granted, that God has this design, this plan, and he chooses whom he will, and most of us are just ordinary people. We have to see ourselves in that light and in that context to understand what community means.

In treating community, Eberhard Arnold starts out by making quite clear something that I don't think is clear enough right now. The big thing today is community. People think in terms of community and also in terms of personal fulfillment, and these are good things. But at the same time, with this great ferment about community, there is a danger. Let me give you an example.

I noticed in the ecumenical field that something strange suddenly started to happen about five or six years ago, just about the time of the opening of the Council.[2] Protestants who disagreed with others of their denomination would come to us, and we who disagreed with other Catholics would go to them. So you found Baptists and Catholics and Presbyterians and Episcopalians who were discontented with their own bunch huddling together in a new group. This is something that tends to happen. As we open up to more people outside the old community, we tend to form other communities. You find grounds of sympathy; people with a new look and a whole new background, and you are stimulated by the first contacts and perhaps you become more involved with them than with your own community. This happens and actually is normal.

The reason for it is probably because we are also in the midst of swinging away from an old situation in which community was rather abstract and what you really had was an organized institution instead of a real community. You had a lot of rules and everything was all set and people did the same thing at the same time and were in the same place at the same time and acted as a community, and probably there was a great deal of charity present in that way of life. But it was also quite possible in this perfect institution to hide an almost total absence of true community. It did cut down on big problems but in a way it created even bigger ones. The fact that everything was so much like a machine made it possible to go through all the motions without any real love or, at least, without any deep personal love for the people you lived with.

At the point I am describing, say ten years ago, people suddenly realized that there was a paralysis in the institutional community; that it was static and even a little bit false and liable to breed all sorts of odd things. Instead of deep personal love, you had sentimental attachments. It was all part of that old picture where life was so closed in and people tended to develop mushy attachments instead of real love. When things suddenly opened up and everyone was getting back into more normal contacts, there was a very strong reaction. People felt, "Here is a healthy community—this is real." And it was more real than the old institutional community, but it was not the real thing, not the community that Christ came to build. As Eberhard Arnold says, there is more to community than just personal fulfillment and sociability.

There is something deeper, and what Arnold does first is to point up the fact that there is a basic optimism about natural community which tends to ignore the struggle of life and death in us. What he wants to stress is the fact that community is not built by man; it is built by God. It is God's work, and the basis of community is not just sociability, but faith. This is what we really need to see very clearly, because it is very important…

At the other extreme you have the story about two old hermits who never quarreled, the idyllic community.[3] It is a screwball story, an exaggeration, but there are two points to it. Most important – the real theological content of the story – is that what really starts fighting is possessions. And people get into fights by preferring things to people. This is well developed in Christian theology, and therefore for us, the importance of detachment from things, the importance of poverty, is that we are supposed to be free from things that we might prefer to people. You can extend that to any limits you like – wherever things have become more important than people, we are in trouble. That is the crux of the whole matter. Figure it out for yourself!

One of the Greek Fathers, Saint Maximus, has an interesting development of this which at one time I wrote up as a basic theology of peace and non-violence. He takes this point and works it up to show how the root of war is in preferring possessions to human values and money to human beings, which is absolutely true. If you look at the war in Vietnam – or any other war – you can really see the heart of the matter. It is investments and material interests that are at stake for the most part, although we certainly do want to protect freedom. That is our expressed desire, but in fact what is happening is that a great number of people are being killed and a great deal of money is being made on it. That's how it actually ends up, which shows there is something wrong with it.

To get back to our proposition, what God wills is the construction of community in Christ, and our job — one of our big responsibilities — is to build community in any way we can. But it must be a real community, in every possible way, remembering the prior objective right of our own community in which we have vows, because that means that we are obliged first to the people we are living with. It is like marriage to some extent, viewed in terms of objective obligations.

But that is not our only obligation. Very often we think that the only people we have to love are our neighbors. Perhaps we never see anyone else to love. But no, we do have to love others and we want to love others and community must extend beyond our own community. The pattern seems to me to be this: in your particular case people come here to find a group of people who love one another. They don't come here merely to see you as individuals; they come to see you as a community of love. If they are going to find grace and help, it isn't so much from each one of you as an individual, but from the grace that is present in a community of love.

However we look at it, we have this obligation to build community; it isn't just an obligation to one another but to all those who come to us. They need to find true community here, and that is the best thing we can give them.

Here is another quotation from Saint Paul's great epistle to the Ephesians, the one on the mystical body. It is really a tremendous one to meditate on in this connection. I am always quoting it to show how community and contemplation and understanding the mystery of Christ are all linked together.

Do not forget, then, that there was a time when you were pagans physically, termed the Uncircumcised by those who speak of themselves as the Circumcision by reason of a physical operation; do not forget, I say, that you had no Christ and were excluded from membership of Israel, aliens with no part in the covenants with their Promise; you were immersed in this world, without hope and without God. But now in Christ Jesus, you that used to be so far apart from us have been brought very close, by the blood of Christ. For he is the peace between us, and has made the two into one and broken down the barrier which used to keep them apart, actually destroying in his own person the hostility caused by the rules and decrees of the Law. This was to create one single New Man in himself out of the two of them and by restoring peace through the cross, to unite them both in a single Body and reconcile them with God. In his own person he killed the hostility. Later he came to bring the good news of peace, peace to you who were far away and peace to those who were near at hand. Through him, both of us have in the one Spirit our way to come to the Father.

So you are no longer aliens or foreign visitors: you are citizens like all the saints, and part of God's household. You are part of a building that has the apostles and prophets for its foundations, and Christ Jesus himself for its main cornerstone. As every structure is aligned on him, all grow into one holy temple in the Lord; and you too, in him, are being built into a house where God lives, in the Spirit (Eph. 2:11–22).

Paul is speaking of the Greek and the Jew – that there is no longer any division. It is one of the difficult passages of Saint Paul. There is so much packed into it, and here is the idea he is always stressing: that the law created division, but the New Testament has overcome division which was created by the law; there is no longer any Jew or any Greek. In this creation of community, therefore, community is based not on ethnic background, not on whether you are a Jew or go to the synagogue, but on the love of persons in Christ, personal relationships in Christ, and it isn't based on nationality or class. And this is where Christians fail so often today.

A politician can go around saying he stands for God, when what he really stands for is racism, and so racism becomes equated with Christianity. This is idolatry, it is turning things inside out. And it is the same with nationalism – people say we will equate our national outlook with Christianity, and suddenly all these things which have nothing at all to do with Christianity become identified with Christianity. This is a serious problem because it is a great scandal to people who have trouble with faith today. They say, "If this man is really a Christian, how can I be a Christian?"

I do want to emphasize the fact that, in himself, on the cross, Christ destroyed the hostility that was created by all these divisions. There again is what community means for us, destroying division by the cross. In other words, we must be bigger than divisions. There will still remain ethnic differences, but they no longer make any difference in Christ. I think that where the real trouble comes is that we have a tendency—it's a sort of American myth—to think that this is all very simple and natural. All you have to do is follow your natural good tendencies and it is all taken care of. It isn't. It isn't automatic, it has to be done by God. It is a work of God.

As Eberhard Arnold says, we really do experience in ourselves, at the same time as the power of Christ, the power of the cross to create community. Yet we also find in ourselves everything that goes against community, and we have to be completely aware of this fact. We are and we are not communal people. It is taken for granted that we are all really sociable. But we are and we aren't. We are also weak and selfish, and there is in us this struggle between trust and mistrust, where we all believe and don't believe. We trust some people and we distrust other people. We are, in other words, full of ambivalence, and we must take this into account. Things are in reality so much more complicated. We assume that we are perfectly open and trusting, and then suddenly we discover that we aren't… What we tend to do is to deny this, repress it; we don't like to face it. But we just have to face the fact that sometimes we get darned mad at people, we get worked up about it and we do our best not to show it, but there it is. You cannot possibly live a religious life realistically unless you realize that this is going on all the time.

The reason we repress our feelings is that they cause anxiety. If I admit to myself that I feel mad and angry, then right away I think what will this lead to? We will be fighting like cats and dogs for months to come, if I show my real feelings. What are you to do? Where are you going to go for help? You go to God. In other words, instead of basing our confidence on our ability to repress these feelings, and keep them out of sight, what we have to do is to take a whole new attitude and say, "All right, I have these feelings and I know they are there. I am sorry about them, but the grace of Christ can fix it, the grace of Christ in me and the grace of Christ in my brother and sister." It isn't just that I have the grace – the point is that the community has the grace. There is sufficient grace to solve all your problems in the ordinary human way – at least *deal* with them – though not to be without them. You have to work at it all the time, but there is this solution. So rejoice; but realize that you do have some work to do…

Let's read a little bit of Eberhard Arnold and what he says about this problem:

God is the source of life. On him and through him our common life is built up and led time and again through cataclysmic struggles to final victory. It is an exceedingly dangerous way, a way of deep suffering. It is a way that leads straight into the struggle for existence and the reality of a life of work, into all the difficulties created by the human character. And yet, just this is our deepest joy: to see clearly the eternal struggle — the indescribable tension between life and death, man's position between heaven and hell — and still to believe in the overwhelming power of life, the power of love to overcome, and the triumph of truth, because we believe in God.

I think that is a pretty inspiring statement. We must believe in community and believe that in God all this is possible. Eberhard Arnold continues:

This faith is not a theory for us; neither is it a dogma, a system of ideas, or a fabric of words, nor a cult or an organization. Faith means receiving God himself — it means being overwhelmed by God. Faith is the strength that enables us to go this way. It helps us to find trust again and again when, from a human point of view, the foundations of trust have been destroyed.

This whole question of believing in God, of trusting in one another and yet knowing that trust can fall and can be rebuilt, all this is part of our life.

Then Arnold makes a statement which I think is extreme. He says, "Admittedly, with our present nature, without God, we humans are incapable of community." That is going too far; it is pessimism. But a statement like this nevertheless has value because, even though it may be exaggerated, it points to the fact that we really need God, and it is the need of grace that Arnold is bringing out.

> Temperamental mood-swings, possessive impulses...all these place seemingly insurmountable obstacles in the way of true community. But with faith we cannot be deluded into thinking that these realities are decisive.

That is the great point. Suppose all these things are there, and supposing it is tough, the thing that faith does is to make a final judgment. Apply this to a marriage problem. Supposing a man discovers his wife has been unfaithful to him. This is one of the tragic kinds of violation of trust in life. It destroys people. So, this husband finds out. If he is the kind of person who says, "This is the end," that is a solution. From the moment a flaw is discovered, finished! That's the end. It is just the opposite with Christ. Even the greatest fault is forgivable. Everything is forgivable.

> Here it becomes abundantly clear that the realization of true community, the actual building up of a communal life, is impossible without faith in a higher Power. In spite of all that goes wrong, people try again and again to put their trust either in human goodness (which really does exist) or in the force of law. But all their efforts are bound to come to grief when faced with the reality of evil.

Again, this is quite strong, but the conclusion rings true: "The only power that can build true community is faith in the ultimate mystery of the Good, faith in God."

The ultimate thing is that we build community not on our love but on God's love, because we do not really have that much love ourselves, and that is the real challenge of the religious life. It puts us in a position where sometimes natural community is very difficult. People are sent here and there, and often very incompatible people are thrown together. Groups of people who would never have chosen to be together in an ordinary human way find themselves living together. It is a test of faith. It puts God's love to the test and it is meant to. It is what Saint Paul means. It isn't just a question of whether you are building community with people that you naturally like, it is also a question of building community with people that God has brought together.

What is tested in community is faith. It is not so much a question of who's right, but do we believe? I think that is the real issue. Of course there are problems, but you put them all together and work them out on the basis and in the context of faith. Faith is first, and the only one who

is right is God. No one of us knows precisely
what God wants. What we have to do is believe
in the power of his love. This power is given to
us in proportion as we work together to find
out what the score is, and then, if we do get
together and decide on something – even if it is
mistaken – if it is done in good faith, the power
of God's love will be in it. We are going to make
mistakes, but it really doesn't matter that much.

Community, politics, and contemplation

I want to talk a little bit more about community because in the church today you have a very strong and active movement that you run into everywhere, in which a whole lot of people – a minority but a very influential minority of whom I know many – say that there is only one real community in existence today and that is the community which is concerned with the problems of under-privileged people, that the only practical way of handling this is revolution, and that Christianity therefore equals revolution.

People talk in this way, and there is going to be trouble because they don't really know what they are talking about. They are all good, middle-class people, and all of a sudden they are talking about revolution.

There is a temptation now of looking for community when you are concerned over political things. After all, you can't avoid it really, you have to be concerned about the world and about politics in some way. But on the other hand, just aligning yourself with somebody else's movement is not necessarily the answer. A good Quaker friend of mine, who was a friend of Martin Luther King, was very much involved with Civil Rights in the South in an absolutely disinterested and dedicated way. She and her husband became involved in a demonstration in Washington. They had absolutely the highest motives, but they joined up with some activists who didn't seem to have the highest motives at all, and they found themselves forced by these people into a weird situation in which they were all arrested. They had been forced to break a law they never intended to break and didn't want to break, so that they could be used and the activists could say, "So-and-so was arrested on our side."

In other words, when you start dealing with people of this sort you are not dealing with community in any Christian sense; you are dealing with a bunch of operators and they have their reasons, but they are in power politics, and this is dangerous…You really have to know what the score is.

I personally think that we should be in between; we shouldn't be on the conservative side and we shouldn't be on the radical side – we should be Christians. We should understand the principles that are involved and realize that we can't get involved in anything where there is not true Christian fellowship. You do have a great deal of good will in these movements and you do have a kernel of desire for community, but power takes priority. The power play is the important thing, and you come up against not love but loveless means. Most activists do not go in for naked violence yet, but they will. In other words, there are ways and means to force people to go in a certain direction. That is okay, that is politics, you might say. If you are a politician you need to know about it and deal with it, but we have to stay out of it.

Writing in the 1920s in Germany, Eberhard Arnold was caught between the Nationalists and the Communists. The Nationalists, who later became the Nazis, represented an absolutely brutal type of community which is simply racism – just crude emotion, lining everybody up and marching them off. This is a sort of massive, fanatical community which I am afraid we are going to see more of in this country. I don't think the whole country will ever be behind it, but some people will be scared and will want to protect their property, and people at the other end will be mixed up in so-called revolutionary action, and we are going to be caught in between.

Arnold saw all this and what he concluded is the position that I pretty well agree with, too – it is the Spirit who is above both these positions, and we have to keep above them, too. We have to be where love is, and it is really the harder position, but it is also the creative position, and the constructive position. It is the kind of position taken by Gandhi.

It is not an idealistic position just because Gandhi took it. I edited and wrote a preface for a little book of quotations from Gandhi on non-violence, and perhaps it is good to remember it because it all tends to get lost now. Non-violence has become all fouled-up and is turning into a sort of semi-violence. But the basic thing Gandhi said, and it has proved absolutely right, is that you can't have any real non-violence unless you have faith in God. If it isn't built on God, it isn't going to work, it isn't going to be real. Gandhi said this, and Martin Luther King picked it up and carried it on. So there you have the spiritual approach, and it was based on asceticism. Gandhi primarily used to fast and use spiritual means. So what we have to do is try to recognize this temptation to seek community in all sorts of power movements, as so many are doing, and to maintain our position in a Christian community – a community built by God.

It is just this situation that Arnold is speaking of when he says that revolutions, communes, and idealistic or reform-oriented movements show both their longing for community and their incapacity for community. What does he mean by revolutions, communes, and idealistic or reform-oriented movements? Maybe he is referring to vegetarians, or to people like the hippies. The hippies are in many ways real good kids. They manifest a desire for community and yet a kind of incapacity for it, so they sort of float around in groups.

I didn't tell you about this hippie down at Christ in the Desert [a monastery], a really lovely guy. He is not just an ordinary hippie; I think he is deeper. He met me at the plane when I went there, and he had this really long hair, with a red leather thong like an Indian to keep it from falling in his eyes while he was driving. A very nice guy. He had this beat-up old Volkswagen station wagon with a stove in the back and a bed where he lived. He was towing a plaster mixer and I asked him, "What have you got that for?" He said, "I figured I was going to do something for the monks, and I am going to work for them for a year and make them bricks for their guest house." He just decided to do that. He is not necessarily a Christian, but he is living at the monastery, and he wants to help the monks out.

He wants a place to think, so he's got his Volkswagen back in the canyon under a tree, and he makes these bricks. He is just absolutely the nicest guy you ever saw. We rode all the way up to Albuquerque, up to the monastery, and all he wanted to talk about was meditation. How do you meditate? What do you do and what do the Hindus do? What do the Buddhists do? He was interested in prayer, and he told me all about his life, how he had been in the army and finally realized that it wasn't making any sense. Now he wanted to find out what it was all about so he went to live in a canyon in his Volkswagen...

At The Redwoods [California] there are some wonderful hippies. As soon as they moved into the area and found out there was a monastery, they all came over and brought food. In fact, they have had a couple of parties there, in the garage, with everyone playing guitars and singing, and the hippies each one doing his own thing, playing what he could play, and they all enjoyed it. This is an example of the desire for community which is all around.

Eberhard Arnold says, "All revolutions, all communes and idealistic or reform-oriented movements, force us to recognize again and again that one thing alone can quicken our faith in the Good: the clear example of action born of truth, when both action and word are one in God," and of course one in Christ; our Lord on the cross is both word and act of God, giving the foundation. "We have only one weapon against the depravity that exists today – the weapon of the Spirit, which is constructive work carried out in the fellowship of love." This is the real basis of community, he says.

Then he takes up the idea that we can't be sentimental about community. It really means working together:

> We do not acknowledge sentimental love, love without work. Nor do we acknowledge dedication to practical work if it does not daily give proof of a heart-to-heart relationship between those who work together, a relationship that comes from the Spirit. The love of work, like the work of love, is a matter of the Spirit.

He writes really well on community life; it is realistic and basic, and the presence of the Spirit is proved by working together in love for a common end.

This, of course, ties in with the great aim of the church today which the Council brought out so strongly in *Gaudium et Spes* [Joy and Hope], and the idea of Teilhard de Chardin[4] – building the new world, collaborating toward the fullness of the maturity, the adulthood of man. Arnold says this:

> We acknowledge Jesus and early Christianity. The early Christians dedicated themselves as much to people's outward needs as to their inner ones. Jesus brought life: he healed sick bodies, resurrected the dead, drove out demons from tormented souls, and carried his message of joy to the poorest of the poor. Jesus' message means the realization of the future invisible kingdom now; it is the promise that ultimately the earth will be won wholly for God.

We are winning the earth completely for God by experiencing the life of love and working together with his power to transform the world. This is a really deep Christian concept which underlies everything that is going on in our life, and that is what contemplation is. Contemplation is the realization of God in our life, not just realization of an idea or something partial, but a realization of the whole thing – the realization that we belong totally to him and he has given himself totally to us. It has all happened and it is going on now.

You have to realize also that you don't really see this. It happens and you see it and you don't. You get glimpses of it, you believe it, your life is based on it, and sometimes it seems to be in complete contradiction or impossible, and yet it is there. It is the place we are always coming back to. What did Saint Paul say?

> That will explain why I, having once heard about your faith in the Lord Jesus and the love that you showed toward all the saints, have never failed to remember you in my prayers and to thank God for you. May the God of our Lord Jesus Christ, the Father of glory, give you a

spirit of wisdom and perception of what is re-
vealed to bring you to full knowledge of him.
May he enlighten the eyes of your mind so that
you can see what hope his call holds for you
(Eph. 1:15–18).

It is all tied up with hope, and hope is what you
don't see. It is a hope which is present but in
invisibility. Somehow you know it and you don't
know it.

> What rich glories he has promised the saints will
> inherit, and how infinitely great is the power he
> has exercised for us believers! This you can tell
> from the strength of his power at work in Christ,
> when he used it to raise him from the dead and
> make him sit at the right hand, in heaven, far
> above every sovereignty, authority, power or
> domination (Eph. 1:18–21).

This is very important. When you get into Saint
Paul, every once in a while you get a lot of power,
authority, and domination, and we tend to slide
right through that. But it is very important,
because prayer is our real freedom. It is libera-

tion from the alienation that I have been talking about.

It is in prayer that we are truly and fully ourselves and we are not under any other power, authority, or domination. We have to see what that means.

> He has put all things under his feet and made him, as the ruler of everything, the head of the Church, which is his body, the fullness of him who fills the whole creation (Eph. 1:22–23).

You have to spend your whole life going over and over again through a passage like this. It is the only way you can ever get anywhere. You don't just read it a few times and then read it with a commentary. You keep coming back to it, and maybe after fifty years of chewing on it you begin to see what it really means.

Notes
to Merton's talks

[1] The Abbey of Our Lady of Gethsemani, the Trappist monastery in Kentucky which Merton entered in 1941 and where he remained as a monk (except when traveling) until his death in 1968.

[2] Merton is referring here to the Second Vatican Council (1962–65), which sought to promote spiritual renewal within the Catholic Church. Its wide-ranging reforms included modification of the liturgy, support for ecumenism, and condemnation of anti-Semitism.

[3] Two Desert Fathers had been living together as hermits for many years and had never gotten into a fight. One of them said to the other, "Why don't we do like everybody else in the world and get into a fight?" The other fellow said, "O.K., how do you do it?" He said, "Well, fights start over possessions, owning something exclusively so that the other fellow can't have it. Let's look around and get ourselves a posses-

sion and then have a fight over it." So he found a brick and said, "I will put this brick between us, and I will say, 'This is my brick,' and you will immediately say, 'No, it is mine,' and then we will get into a fight." So the man gets the brick and puts it down between the two of them and says, "This is my brick." And the other says, "Well, brother, if it is your brick, take it." From *Thomas Merton in Alaska,* p. 86.

[4] Pierre Teilhard de Chardin, 1881–1955, French scientist and Catholic theologian.

Postscript
by the editors

Though Eberhard Arnold is relatively unknown today, in his lifetime (1883–1935) his impact was felt by hundreds of thousands. As his writing amply testifies, he had a unique insight and a deep understanding of the church as the living Body of Christ.

In 1920, venturing into an unknown future – and leaving wealth, security, and an increasingly visible career – Eberhard, his wife Emmy, and their five children moved from Berlin to Sannerz, a village in central Germany, where they founded a small community of families and singles on the basis of early church practices as described in the New Testament.

Despite persecution by the Nazis, the turmoil of World War II, and times of spiritual decline, the community known as the Bruderhof ("place of brothers") survived. Today it continues in some two dozen locations around the world.

We are small and insignificant in numbers (approximately 2,500), yet we believe our task is of utmost importance: to follow Jesus' teachings in the Sermon on the Mount and to witness to his gospel in a society which has turned against him. We come from many countries and walks of life, but we are all brothers and sisters in Christ.

The basis of our communal life is the living Word of Christ: we simply try to follow his teachings, especially concerning brotherly love, love of enemies, mutual service, nonviolence and the refusal to bear arms, sexual purity, and faithfulness in marriage.

We have no private property, but share everything in common, the way the first Christians did as recorded in the Book of Acts, chapters 2 and 4. Each member gives his or her talents, time, and effort wherever they are needed. We meet daily for prayer, worship, singing, and decision making.

We earn our living chiefly by manufacturing and selling "Community Playthings," a line of play equipment and furniture for schools and day-care centers, and "Rifton Equipment for People with Disabilities."

Our children attend the community day care, school, and high school. Further education takes place outside the community.

We welcome guests at all our communities. Adult membership, which is voluntary, follows believer's baptism and a period of discernment before making a life-time commitment.

Mission has always been a vital focus of our activity, but not in the sense of trying to gain members for "our" church. Far more important to us are the connections we make with others who truly seek to be obedient to God's will in their lives, no matter what their label.

With Eberhard Arnold we affirm: "This planet, the earth, must be conquered for a new kingdom, a new social order, a new unity, a new joy. This joy comes to us from the God who is the God of love, who is the Spirit of peace and of unity and community. This is the message Jesus brings. And we must have the faith and the certainty that his message is valid still today."

The Editors

For more information about our communities, or to arrange a visit, please write to one of the addresses below:

Darvell Community
Robertsbridge, E. Sussex
TN32 5DR UK
(01580) 883 300

Woodcrest Community
2032 Rte 213
PO Box 903
Rifton NY 12471, USA
845 658 7700

Danthonia Community
4188 Gwydir Highway
Elsmore NSW 2360 AUS
02 6723 2213

or visit www.bruderhof.com.

Emmy Arnold

A Joyful Pilgrimage
My Life in Community

In the tumultuous aftermath of the First World War, thousands of young Germans defied the social mores of their parents – and the constricting influence of the established churches – in search of freedom, social equality, nature, and community. Hiking clubs were formed and work camps organized, and hundreds of rural folk schools and communes sprang up across the country. In the 1930s Nazism swallowed this so-called Youth Movement virtually whole.

A Joyful Pilgrimage is the engaging story of a remnant that survived: the Bruderhof, a 75-year-old community that began when the author and her husband abandoned their affluent Berlin suburb to start a new life and "venture of faith."

Lyn Baker, Logos Journal
Details in subdued and undramatic fashion how ordinary middle-class Christians were spurred by the Holy Spirit and the decadence of their culture to become lowly, dependent, and centered on God.

Clarence Jordan, author, *The Cottonpatch Gospels*
A moving story…and an amazing continuation of the Book of Acts.

Thomas Merton
Very moving…Emmy Arnold's story is a simple and direct account of a Christian life stripped to the essentials.

184 pp., softcover, 1998

Eberhard Arnold

God's Revolution

Judging by much of what is bought and read these days, many people see discipleship as the religious route to personal fulfillment. This anthology approaches discipleship as revolution: as a transformation that begins within but has power to change every aspect of life.

Arnold's vision of peace and justice is a vision for the whole world, but it is rooted in his firm belief that the new order of God's coming kingdom will be realized only insofar as we let it transform our personal lives.

Jim Wallis, *Sojourners*
A much needed corrective to a church that has lost the vital, biblical connection between belief and obedience. Arnold's clear call to follow Jesus offers both simple and prophetic pastoral instruction to help us understand what discipleship might look like in the modern world.

Mark O. Hatfield
A truly inspiring account of individual and group commitment to an authentic Christian alternative. I recommend this book enthusiastically.

232 pp., softcover, 1997

J. Heinrich Arnold

Discipleship

Foreword by
Henri J. M. Nouwen

Written over a span of several decades, *Discipleship* offers hard-won insights into the challenges of following Christ in the nitty-gritty daily life. Many of the 300 short pieces (from Arnold's writings, letters, and talks) are answers to specific needs or problems. Others address basic questions of Christian practice and belief. Still others grapple with broader themes such as world suffering, salvation, and the coming of the kingdom of God. All of them are marked by a spirit of quiet certainty and compassion, and all of them will give fresh hope to any who find themselves lonely or disheartened in the daily search to follow Christ.

Mother Teresa, Sisters of Charity
I pray for all who read this book that they may come to follow Jesus more closely in their whole lives. He has not called us to be successful, but to be faithful.

Sister Helen Prejean, Dead Man Walking
Discipleship is not simply a book. It is a cry from the heart of a man passionately alive for God and the work of God. Arnold's words blow on the simmering coals of our hearts and set us on fire for Christ.

304 pp., softcover, 1994

Contents